Sports Stars

HULK HOGAN

Eye of the Tiger

By Barry Janoff

 CHILDRENS PRESS ®

CHICAGO

Cover photograph: Focus on Sports Incorporated
Inside photographs courtesy of the following:
Focus on Sports Incorporated, pages 6, 14, 16, 18, 21,
24, 26, 35, 37, 39, and 41
AP/Wide World Photos, pages 8, 12, 28, 30, and 32

Library of Congress Cataloging in Publication Data

Janoff, Barry.
  Hulk Hogan: eye of the tiger.

  (Sport stars)
  Summary: A biography of the heavyweight champion of
the World Wrestling Foundation.
  1. Hogan, Hulk, 1955-   —Juvenile literature.
2. Wrestlers—United States—Biography—Juvenile literature.
[1. Hogan, Hulk, 1955-   . 2. Wrestlers.] I. Title.
GV1196.H64J36 1986   796.8'12'0924 [B] [92] 85-28047
ISBN 0-516-04356-0

    4 5 6 7 8 9 10 R 95 94 93 92

Sports Stars

HULK HOGAN

Eye of the Tiger

Professional wrestling is a colorful and fascinating event. Many people around the world are fans of wrestling. There is a lot of action and excitement at every wrestling match.

There are many professional wrestlers. But the most exciting wrestler is Hulk Hogan. Hulk Hogan is the heavyweight champion of the World Wrestling Federation. That means he is the best heavyweight wrestler in the world.

Hulk before he appeared on "Saturday Night's Main Event" on NBC-TV

"When I was little, my father took me to see a wrestling match," says Hulk. "When I saw it I was turned on. I said, 'one day I'm going to be the World Wrestling Federation heavyweight champion.'

"And that's exactly what happened. If you want to be somebody, you can do it if you want it that bad. But you have to put your blood, sweat, and tears into it. You have to believe in it."

Becoming the heavyweight champion was not easy. Hulk was big when he was growing up.

But many people thought he was too quiet to become a wrestler. Others thought he wasn't strong enough.

"But I dedicated myself to my training," Hulk remembers. "I'm not a bodybuilder. I went into weight training. I went into the gym for some heavy-duty weight and conditioning training. And I watched my diet. I ate my vitamins and said my prayers."

When he was 12 years old, Hulk was 6 feet tall. He weighed 192 pounds. But he was not strong enough to become a professional wrestler.

Today he is 6 feet 8 inches tall. He weighs 305 pounds.

Hulk Hogan has been a wrestler for 10 years. Hulk appeared in the movie, *Rocky III*, in 1982. The movie stars Sylvester Stallone as Rocky, a boxer. Hulk plays the part of Thunderlips, a wrestler. He beats Rocky in the ring. After the movie, Hulk became popular.

The theme song of the movie was "Eye of the Tiger." Now, whenever he wrestles, Hulk Hogan's theme song is "Eye of the Tiger."

When he first became a wrestler, Hulk worked under the name of Sterling Golden. That was because of his long, blond hair. He was considered a bad guy. Fans would come to boo him. They liked to see him lose.

In "Rocky III," Hulk played the role of Thunderlips.

But soon, Hulk met Freddie Blassie. He is a wrestling manager and promoter. He worked with Hulk. He changed Hulk's image. Now Hulk is a good guy. Fans from around the world come to cheer Hulk. They come to see him win.

Hulk's fans are loyal and dedicated. A special word was coined to describe how they feel: Hulkamania!

"What is Hulkamania?" Hulk Hogan smiles. "It's like a fever. It's like a plague, but a good plague. Everywhere you go, everything you do has got to be positive.

Hulk is the heavyweight champion of the World Wrestling Federation.

"Everything I do is real. My fans get off on that. I live this day and night. It's me. It's my ability to drive others to make something out of their lives."

Hulkamania does not exist only in the wrestling ring. For Hulk Hogan, it means being the best you can be—all the time.

"Once, there was this young boy who had bad luck with his health," remembers Hulk's mother, Ruth Hogan. "He was real bad off in a hospital in Pennsylvania. His hero was Hulk Hogan. Hulk was his idol. Hulk heard about the boy and sent him an autographed picture. The boy was thrilled. Hulk always does things like that."

Hulk is the best he can be—all the time.

That is part of Hulkamania as well.

Hulk considers himself a native of Venice Beach, California. Many athletes train there. So Venice Beach also is known as Muscle Beach.

Before he became Hulk Hogan, his name was Terry. He lived with his parents and two brothers in Tampa Bay, Florida.

Hulk's first love was baseball. He played in the Little League, Colt League, and Pony League. He was a pitcher. When he was 12, he was the star on his team. He helped his teammates to win the city championship.

Fans from around the world come to cheer Hulk.

Hulk's second favorite sport when he was growing up was bowling. He and a friend, Vic Petitt, won a doubles championship for the city of Tampa.

Hulk injured his arm when he was 15. He was a pitcher in Little League. During a game he felt something tear in his elbow. His doctor thought that Hulk's arm would never be strong again. That is when he started working out. His coach thought he could have been a major league pitcher. But the injury ended his baseball career.

Hulk's parents bought him a guitar when he was young. He was always interested in music.

When he got the guitar, he was able to express himself through his music.

"From the time he was 13 all the way through college he played guitar," says Hulk's mother. "He had three or four bands. The last one was called Rukus.

"One day, Hulk's father and I walked into a fancy club. Hulk and his band were dressed up in tuxedos. They were playing songs from Broadway shows, but rock-and-roll style. It was really beautiful."

Hulk went to the University of South Florida. He majored in music and business.

In the movie, "Rocky III," Thunderlips beats Rocky in the ring.

Hulk's love of music is strong even today. He sits in with musicians whenever he can. In 1984 he played a song called, "Itchiban" on the bass guitar. That is Japanese for Number One. The song was a hit in Japan and was on top of the charts.

That, too, is part of Hulkamania.

"People ask me if wrestling is real," Hulk says. "It's real. I've had my nose broken. I've had black eyes. I had water on the knee and torn muscles.

"I live wrestling day and night. Blood, sweat, and tears is the way I live this. The people get off on that. They believe in it. I believe in it. That's why the Hulkster is Number One at what he does: pinning people in the center of the ring.

"When I was a tiny little Hulkster, my father took me to the wrestling matches. I would watch those guys—a one-on-one confrontation. The ultimate physical confrontation. No helmets. No shoulder pads. No tennis racquets. They were butting heads. Locking up like big guns."

When Hulk decided to make wrestling his life, he thought back to the days when he and his father would watch wrestlers. Wrestlers like

Bruno Sammartino

Bruno Sammartino and Gorilla Monsoon. They were champions. Hulk wanted to be a champion, too.

"I wanted to be big, rough, and tough in the ring," says Hulk. "I wanted to be so big that the other wrestlers, my peers, would be afraid of me. I wanted to be so big that they would have to stick me in a steel cage. They could put me in the ring. And I would scare the other wrestlers without even doing a thing."

Hulk never got his steel cage. But he worked out with weights day and night. He developed his muscles. In the ring, he won all his important matches. Soon, he earned a chance to wres-

Gorilla Monsoon

tle for the heavyweight championship of the world.

On January 24, 1984, Hulk Hogan met the Iron Sheik, a wrestler from Iran. They met in Madison Square Garden in New York. The Sheik had won the heavyweight championship a month before his match with Hulk. The Sheik is considered one of wrestling's bad guys.

The fans wanted to see Hulk win. They wanted the Sheik to lose. They were not disappointed. Hulk's theme song, "Eye of the Tiger," played. Hulk used his strength and defeated the Sheik. The match took less than eight minutes. When it

Mr. T shakes hands with Hulk.

was over, Hulk Hogan was the champion of the world.

"On that night, my dream of becoming the World Wrestling Federation heavyweight champ became a reality," Hulk recalls. "It was a super feeling. I worked hard to earn the title. It was my goal, and I went after it."

Madison Square Garden is a famous arena. The New York Knicks play basketball there. The New York Rangers play hockey there. Many important concerts and events take place there every month.

Another exciting event took place there on March 31, 1985. On that day, every seat was

Hulk and Mr. T conduct a news conference in New York's Madison Square Garden before "WrestleMania."

filled with fans. They came to see an event called WrestleMania.

The star of WrestleMania was Hulk Hogan. His partner was Mr. T. Mr. T is on the television show, "The A Team." Hulk and Mr. T were teamed against two of wrestling's bad guys. They were Rowdy Roddy Piper and Paul (Mr. Wonderful) Orndorff.

Many famous people were there to see this event. Cyndi Lauper, who sings "Girls Just Wanna Have Fun," was there. Muhammad Ali, the former boxing heavyweight champion of the world, was there. Billy Martin, manager of baseball's New York Yankees, was there.

Hulk was Cyndi Lauper's escort when she received a Grammy for best new artist.

But something else was important to Hulk and Mr. T. That was the 24,000 fans who came to cheer them to victory.

"Eye of the Tiger" began to play. The match began. When it ended, Hulk and Mr. T were winners. The crowd never sat down. For the whole match, everyone was cheering for Hulk Hogan and Mr. T.

Hulkamania had reached a new peak.

"I am the World Wrestling Federation heavyweight champion. I go out there to win wrestling matches," Hulk says. "I don't go out there to break bones or hurt people or anything like that. I take people out into the middle of the ring. I try to beat them fair and square, one, two, three."

Hulk Hogan has had much success in the ring. He wants to defend his heavyweight title for as long as he can. Many people think he can beat the record held by Bruno Sammartino. He was the heavyweight champion for almost 12 years.

But Hulk has other projects. One is the television cartoon show that started in September, 1985. It is called "Hulk's Rock 'n' Wrestling." The show features many of wrestling's top stars as cartoon characters, including Hulk Hogan.

It isn't easy to beat Hulk. That is why he is the heavyweight champion.

The show tells how these wrestlers work hard in the ring. It tells how they help people when they are not in the ring.

One story shows how Hulk and his friends helped to cheer up a young boy who was in the hospital. The story is like real life. Hulk does visit hospitals and cheer up young boys and girls.

Hulk also has other plans. He has been contracted to star in other television shows as well as movies. There are many Hulk Hogan products, including T-shirts, dolls, books, and games. There is a videotape called *Hulkamania*. It is a video of Hulk's best wrestling matches.

Hulk is successful on TV as well as in the ring. He is a real showman.

But there is a lot more to Hulk Hogan than just wrestling. "People who don't know me call me a monster," Hulk says. "I take monster as a compliment. It doesn't mean something ugly to me. It means I can't be stopped. It means other wrestlers can't believe how big I am.

"I am the best at both things I do—wrestling and theatrics. When I go out there and shake my hair and flex my muscles, you hear people scream and yell. Twenty thousand people yell when I flex my arm."

Hulk's image is very important to him. He knows that a lot of his fans are young boys and girls. When he does something, they watch him.

Mr. T and Hulk Hogan make a good team.

They often follow his example.

Hulk Hogan makes it very clear to all his fans. He is very careful about his health. He is very careful about what he eats. He never has had, and never will have, a drug problem.

"It's hard for me to explain what it's like to be the Hulk," he says. "When you are the world champion, you are the Number One wrestler. You are the one the fans come to see. You can't just be a big, dumb wrestler. You have to be smart.

The fans throw their paper cups at the "bad guy," Hulk's opponent.

"My main man is Mr. T. As Mr. T says, 'when you're a champion, you dedicate yourself to something.' I have dedicated myself to this day and night. I have to answer to myself for everything that I do."

Today, Hulk is as big a star as one can be. He makes more than $1 million a year.

He is still a bachelor. He doesn't smoke or drink. He always wears a large crucifix around his neck. "I have God in my corner," he says.

In April 1987, Hulk had to defend his Wrestle-Mania title again. He had won it twice. But this time it was in Pontiac, Michigan, a suburb of Detroit. This time there were more than 93,000 fans there! It was the largest indoor crowd to see a sports event in history.

And this time Hulk had to meet his old enemy, Andre the Giant. Hulk Hogan is very big. But Andre is even bigger. Even so, Hulk amazed everyone by picking up Andre, slamming him to the canvas, and pinning him. Hulk Hogan was still champion.

After a title match in St. Louis in 1990, Hulk kept the WWF title by defeating Randy (Macho Man) Savage.

In the heroes-and-villains world of professional wrestling, Hulk is still the biggest hero of them all. He likes that. Fans like that. The people who run wrestling like that. Hulk is a national star.

CHRONOLOGY

1953—Terry Gene Bollea is born in Tampa Bay, Florida.

1967—Terry leads his Little League baseball team to the city All-Star game championship.

1969—With a friend, Terry wins the Tampa Bay bowling doubles championship.

1970—Terry injures his pitching arm and is forced out of baseball.

1973—He attends the University of South Florida and majors in music and business.

1976—Terry decides to become a professional wrestler. He works under the name Sterling Golden. He meets wrestling manager Freddie Blassie and begins to tour on the wrestling circuit as Hulk Hogan.

1982—Hulk appears with Mr. T in the movie, *Rocky III*, as Thunderlips.

—Hulk changes his image from bad guy to good guy and wrestles to the theme song, "Eye of the Tiger."

1984—Hulk defeats the Iron Sheik at Madison Square Garden to win the World Wrestling Federation heavyweight title, January 24.

1985—Hulk teams with Mr. T at Madison Square Garden. They win the event called WrestleMania, March 31.

—Hulk Hogan appears on the cover of *Sports Illustrated*, April 29.

—Television cartoon show, "Hulk Hogan's Rock 'n' Wrestling," begins, September 14.

1986—Hulk Hogan is the star of WrestleMania II, with football stars such as William (The Regrigerator) Perry included in the show.

1987—WrestleMania III is held in the Pontiac Silverdome. More than 93,000 fans show up to make it the world's largest indoor crowd. The winner? Hulk Hogan again.

1989—Hulk Hogan wins WrestleMania V, and is named the World Heavyweight Champion by the World Wrestling Federation.

1990—Hulk keeps the WWF championship after defeating Randy (Macho Man) Savage in their title match in St. Louis.

ABOUT THE AUTHOR

Barry Janoff has been writing about sports for more than 12 years. He has covered professional, college, and high school sports for numerous publications and has interviewed many of the top athletes in the world. In 1982 he toured Yugoslavia with the U.S. Women's Olympic Basketball team and in 1985 went to Cuba with a men's All-Star basketball team. His work has appeared in *Football Digest, Basketball Digest,* and *Soccer Digest*; CBS Publications; *HOOP,* the official magazine of the National Basketball Association; and the Associated Features series of sports books. He has written another Sports Stars book about Alan Trammell. During the past six years he has written numerous features for the Associated Press. For the past three years he has been Sports Editor for Laurant Publications, which prints a variety of national sports and entertainment magazines and books.